House Built of Rain

House Built of Rain

by Russell Thornton

Harbour Publishing

Published by
Harbour Publishing Co. Ltd., P.O. Box 219,
Madeira Park, BC V0N 2H0
www.harbourpublishing.com

Cover painting by Marusya Sribna
Edited and designed by Silas White
Printed and bound in Canada

Harbour Publishing acknowledges the financial support from the Government of Canada through the Book Publishing Industry Development Program (BPIDP) and the Canada Council for the Arts, and the Province of British Columbia through the British Columbia Arts Council, for its publishing activities.

National Library of Canada Cataloguing in Publication Data

Thornton, Russell
  House built of rain / Russell Thornton.

  Poems.
  ISBN 1-55017-281-6

  I. Title.
PS8589.H565H68 2003   C811'.54   C2003-910188-6
PR9199.3.T485H68 2003

Somehow I hear oarlocks and a rocking rowboat
striking the side of the house. Now it seems
the front door is being tried, the back door. Who is it
rowing around the house in this flood, wanting in?
And now I know it is rain—but it is too late;
a whole new rain has swept in through the rain,
and that rain is a solitary infant journeying
in its tiny vessel, its ark empty except for itself,
come here to nestle at the house. . .

TABLE OF CONTENTS

I

The Eyes of Travel

No one recalls how long ago the last train left,
but the first houses, the houses that went up in a throng
alongside the track when the train first ran,
and are derelict now, seem to cling to the memory.
The houses' creaking front doors, their paint peeling,
are like old, now never-looked-at mirrors,
and the crumbling front porches, the gates and fences,
stare at nothing, like desolate people.

The ones who stepped onto the train and were gone
are still young, still in love, their hearts like liquid light.
Somewhere they are all still on the train,
though none of them know where it is going—
all they know is that they had to become travellers.
Now their hearts, quick and unfailing, are one with the train's rhythm,
their faces, lit torches in an endless night, lead the way.
Now they themselves are the only pair of rails they follow.

If we bring new wood and make repairs,
and if we retouch the town's sad houses,
our own hearts will still be those the loving ones abandoned.
If we gaze after them, and if we praise them,
and our eyes turn bright with exquisite distance,
our eyes will still be the tracks their eyes left behind,
like the sunken tracks sheep make, streaming ahead of us
into the promised land, in the promised land.

My Mother and the Rain

Early in the morning, she wakes the four of us
and marches us into the kitchen—while we rub sleep out of our eyes,
our pajamas awry, our hair sticking out (one particular cowlick
even more pronounced than it is during the day),
the two middle ones on the verge of quiet laughter,
bewildered and canny and secretive all at the same time,
the youngest alert-transparent, taking everything in.
"Wait," she tells us, unlocks the back door
and leads us out onto the porch, along the house wall
under the overhang, where she sits us down together in a row,
drapes a big blanket over us and nestles in. Little looks
go back and forth between us: *Is she what's called crazy?*
Is this a dream we're all having? "Listen," she says.

The rain's falling wildly, roaring down the pipes
that drain the eavestroughs, tap dancing on the porch,
spraying out everywhere like happily splashing-sounding stars;
out at the edge of the tree-filled backyard, the rain's
hushing itself, filling the trees, making the tree branches
heavier and heavier, making them rise as if to embrace the rain.
And rain mist is whispering in the grass, polished steel
rain hoops are spinning and ringing down the back steps
off into the air and onto the grass, and unfamiliar,
ever-metamorphosing bright musical instruments
made of rain are appearing and appearing, while mysterious
half-visible half-human-sized musicians—ghostlike, glowing
and made of mist—play the instruments. Is what we hear and see
what she has meant us to hear and see? All she says is: "Listen."

Later, out in the day, we will be at a bus stop. Those middle two
standing alongside me now next to a post, their four and five year olds'
odd about-to-become-grins on their faces, the youngest
on the bench spilling out of her lap. "Make the bus come, Mom."
She lights a cigarette. Thirty seconds later, like magic,
the bus comes lumbering up. My brothers grinning outright—
and my mother's greenish eyes shining, the rain
falling into the green backyard. Me and my brothers
looking up at her, laughing, and though we don't know it, beginning
the lives we'll have, whatever happens, listening to the same rain.

A Pause

The furnace rumblings and street noises have died;
now it is as if all sound is suspended in an elsewhere
that is the inside of what I am. I remember a night
I ran from a house. The house's spaces
had bulged within me—I sat up in my bed,
still, and straining to listen. Then crept silently
up a long set of basement stairs, closer to the yells
and crashing thuds. I crouched at a doorway and saw
my mother crumpled on the floor, dotted in burns,
her face smudged and over-bright and distorted.
I went lightly, quickly back the way I had come. The blood
caught in my heart became a pure fuel
sweeping me out into the street and into a no-time
opening between my pulse-beats; the block
now had no end, and I ran knocking at front door
after front door, my feet only barely needing
to touch the smooth, glistening, ridiculing lawns.

Then it was years later; I was in a viewless bar
as in the entranceway to my veins. Any new memory
I had gained had left me without my knowing it,
as if it were a song I was unaware had ended.
I saw a woman walk in—who stood and watched me,
seeming to know me, came and sat with me,
and asked me to her small home. And I knew her,
but only as I know her now—in the dream I have of her.
I am a child and am somewhere in my house;
somehow she too is there. I see her as she circles
through the house, circles and finally turns
at a half-open door into a room I do not remember.
She disappears into a darkness. In the dream
I wake unable to move. My flesh is nothing but feeling.
And the night is as much her as anything.
Like a pause in a piece of unknown
and exquisite, anguished music. Like a pause, a pause.

Brothers

One spent nights on the junior high school roof.
My mother had kicked him out when the police told her
he was selling drugs, and before that, selling tires
he stole from gas stations. One stole a teacher's car
from the senior high school parking lot at lunchtime,
got a case of beer, and drove around drunk all afternoon,
then smashed the car's front fender when he reparked it.
One threw a Molotov cocktail into a teacher's home
when the teacher accused him of copying an essay.
The same one beat up his P.E. teacher. One beat up
the leader of a gang. With that gang after him,
he started his own gang, he himself its only member,
and wore a red bandana and red old lady's jacket
to school every day. No one along the gauntlet
that had been set up to stop him touched him.
Each one headed to "alternate school." A year or two,
and the school was the bar, the drunk tank, jail.
But each one changed, and turned himself around.
Here we all are, suddenly in our mid and late thirties,
with everyone fooled. Clean-living, clean-looking,
all of us successful and good middle-class boys.
One a CEO, one a president of marketing. . . all
with pretty partners, nice cars, nice paid-for houses.
And smilers and jokers around a dinner table.
Until something comes out after a beer or glass of wine
too many, a note in a voice, and we are all there in a row
and looking to either side of ourselves at each other,
trying to see the thing looking out of our faces
as out of cold, dark trees it stands at the edge of
yet blends in. Each of us knowing it is there, each of us
ready to kill it, even when we know it is one of us—
though none of us knows which of us it is, only
that it is there and it is a lone, long-absent animal,
starving and afraid and ready to kill, and our father.

Running

I was walking and hurling myself and shouting a taunt
at anyone else who might be out on the street,
then I heard quick footsteps cross behind me,
turned, and saw his face in the streetlamp light—
a sudden mirror shining bright but empty
that immediately siphoned away into blackness—
as I was struck in the head with a two-by-four.
When I had gotten up from the sidewalk, I ran,
ran and brought him down and pinned him,
hit and hit his face, then stood and kicked him
until he lay motionless, soaked in ditch muck.
And when I saw the police car, I veered away
and ran, so ecstatic, I was about to weep.

                                                  Years later,
when I had been struck by a car and flung,
then struck again, and the finally stopped car
let its headlights' brilliance fall over me
where I lay curled up on the road, I simply waited,
able almost to taste the adrenaline, yet calm and still.
I lay there as if I had never been anywhere
except caught in a familiar searching glare
that was as careless of me as of any animal
it reached through softly, making the limbs stiffen,
and as if I had never experienced anything
other than a widening moment of beseeching
when words were said slowly over a hurt body
and the pursuer lifted the weight into his arms
with no memory he could know as his own.

In the Sonora Hills

No town near, no other people, only the soft black sky,
the fiesta of the white molten-looking stars,
the fire we had built like a jostling of spirits,
the encircling naked hills and the vacant nostalgia they carried,
the darkness that curved in bone the length of my spine.
The women had gone off to wait in an old Cadillac,
letting their exquisite nostrils dance at held-out packets of cocaine
like young hens at grain thrown out of the sky.
The one I had hidden away with, imagining that all I wanted
was to be wherever I was with her, the one like a just-lit, dark flame,
the one who knew I would betray her, had betrayed me.
The men had handed me American beer and a bottle,
and turned and stepped away and become vague shapes
discussing in secret voices what they would do with me.
In a part of myself I could not care: I had stepped into an aloneness
where I thought nothing could touch me, nothing,
and whatever they did with me would be all right.
Still, I saw the fire's flames plead with twisting outstretched arms
as if there were somewhere the fire wanted to go
but would never find before it as soon died away
and a whole other fire appeared in its place instantaneously
out of the pure unknowing of the dark.
I heard the women laughing, and calling out the men's names,
and the men rejoined me, tense but still civil, and drank with me,
all seemingly unaware of why they had let me alone.
The hills, the encircling wild hills, forever travelling,
and still not yet here, not yet where they were travelling to,
now showed the first grey touch of morning light.
Back in the car I knew to keep silent,
and the woman, the one who did not look at me again
but scribbled her name on a scrap of paper unnoticed
and placed it in my hand, stayed silent along with the others.
Then we pulled into a deserted gas station, and I knew to get out,
and was blinded by a sudden dazzle of glare and animate dust,
and did not look up as the car spun half around me and was gone.

The Thermos

The backyard garden was not ours,
and I had been told not to play
in among the vegetables,
but did anyway, chancing on
what I would later learn were called
carrots, tomatoes, zucchini.
I was a set of toddler's eyes
filled with the green wet-bright damage
of my mother's look, the unchecked
clear ray of joy in her, the hurt,
the blue ruinous-bright hard rage
of my father's look, the presence
and fineness in him, the being trapped.
I had been born in the centre
of their teenaged and sweet and wild,
painful dream, yet I could only
ever be partly there, as if
I were a ghost no one could name—
though they had cried its name was love.
At the garden's edge, where the neat
planted rows ran out at a fence,
I found an old sealed Thermos
hidden in dirt and tangled grass.
I brought it out into the light,
took off the cup lid, looked far down
along a curved mirror and saw
the whole sky splay out at me then
whirl back down into a dark blue—
dark as if the night were right there
within the brilliant sunny day.
Then it was light again, night-edged
and glittering, smooth and silver,
and lying broken in pieces

in the Thermos' depths—the heaped
pieces of a jigsaw puzzle.
I pulled a piece out and moved it
around, made light flash this way, that,
then trained it on everything
in the yard so it would reveal
how it easily became things,
how it knew all the different
greens, reds and oranges of the garden,
the dark brown of the beer bottles
stacked and scattered on the back porch.
Then I took the puzzle piece
and cut into my calf with it.
For a long moment, I gazed rapt
at the vivid pouring crimson.
Then I began my single scream.
Then I saw my mother running
wide-eyed toward me. Her screaming
and mine joined in a single thick
flow in the air, found my father
far away somewhere and took in
his scream without his knowing it.
It was beautiful, complete.
I stood there with the mirror piece
in my hand. I might have brought out
of my flesh a miracle birth.
It shone unknown light through the blood,
an astonished, astonishing
being made of the three of us.
And it was beautiful. And I screamed.

Magdalena Dawn

Town on the road from nowhere to nowhere,
dust-ridden, air dry as the inside of a gourd rattle.
Someone turns to me out of a sudden
encompassing quietness in the midst of low drone
and tells me there is a festival held here in the fall,
a celebration of the deer and of St. Francis the healer.
But this is the empty centre of the summer,
and the frenzy circling itself everywhere
is only the townspeople holding up the hours.
I came here to nights in the same small bar,
and to days on the same sun-wasted streets,
hoping someone would find me and tell me
why I was here, and give me news of who I was.
So lost from myself I could lick the grease from any pan.
Then a dream: it is as if I have become
the dust of the street. A small shift of air,
and for a few instants, the subtle grains
that have kept her secret reveal her: a woman
in a crowd; in the centre of the crowd
an open space out of which dancers sight the deer.
And I wake having been shown just enough
to know how she is around the edge
of every movement, the edge of every atom.
And the grains, glassy and praying to be filled, are filled,
dust eyes being born again and again,
brightening with her widening, deep gold.

The Holy Rose

Red Rose, proud Rose, sad Rose. . .
    −W.B. Yeats, "To The Rose Upon The Rood Of Time"

"When I'm depressed, I wear red, I don't know why," you once said.
And today you have on a crimson T-shirt under your V-neck sweater.
A few nights ago, I dreamt I had found the way inside the mountain.
I turned the right way between fir trees at last, and entered different air,
a door I had always known had to exist, and the mountain
brought me into its inner dark. A woman was there to meet me,
dressed in feathers and animal skins, beautiful, smiling,
strands of silver in her black hair. She motioned to me to follow.
We entered a chamber, a primitive chapel, decorations,
half-visible, hanging everywhere. The woman's daughter appeared,
stepping out of the deeper dark of an inner passageway.
She went to her mother, spoke with her, then turned,
her eyes lit with untraceable sorrow, and gazed at me,
showing me how much joy was possible. And I asked her her name.
"Roz," she said, a soft smile on red lips, "Rozamonde."
And now here you are, in the light of day, in a rained-on house,
come to this mountain-, tree-, creek- and inlet-turned city
from a faraway other country, and taking off your T-shirt,
and suddenly completely undressed and displaying your pride,
your luxuriant curls and Venus flower. The holy rose in you
lets you be a white blaze that pours wherever I touch it;
and your sadness, a strange bliss; and me, a man who arrives
at a shrine, at imperishable petals, where all desire bows down.

The Day of My Beginning

There's a preamble of a couple of years.
I see it go by in seconds. The two of them
are thirteen, fourteen. My father slides in
beside my mother at the local movie theatre,
puts his arm around her. That's it: she's his
and he's hers. Now they're in school photos:
in the first ones, she's still a laughing child,
his soccer medal strung around her neck;
he's imitating James Dean. From then on,
she's darker-looking, more glittering-looking,
the love-wisdom looking out of her;
he's lost his grin, he's touched the darkness
and loneliness in himself—gone some place
he'll never come back from. Grade eleven,
he's already the doomed drunk who shows up
hammered everywhere, gets expelled,
yells down the school corridors for his woman.
She's running to him. It's a weekday
in the late 1950s. Her parents
will be at work until six. It's a day
of phosphorescent violet low heavens
and balminess in the middle of winter.
Three months from this afternoon,
because of this afternoon, they'll be married.
They're crazily, unstoppably in love. They're
just elastic flesh vessels moving in tandem
with the wild stream of concentrated
radiance swerving through them. They're
in the upstairs room she and her sister share,
rain beginning to dance on the low roof,
rain-music raining down into the room.

I'm hovering above them, I'm entering
the stream quickening its flow within them.
I'm the something that has made her
choose him, and made him choose her—
so it couldn't have been any other way.
I'm the moment they're opening together—
which is calling me without their knowing it
through the perfect sounds of their own names.
I'll have to use whatever amount of spirit I have
to get through the next eight and a half years—
while they take their punishment and watch
what couldn't have lasted between them die.
I'll have to use more spirit than I have
to get through two, three decades after that.
But already, I'm the praise I'll utter.
More than anything, to get through time
I'll have to use the feeling he and she had
in their beginning, before they knew
who they were—even as I rid myself of much
of what I can know of them. I'll have to use
that ecstasy. Already, I'm thanking them
for refusing not to keep me. I'll have to forget
almost more than I can, I'll have to use
the feeling that passed through them into me
and streamed out through my life, which will
make me say thank you, thank you—
as it finds me, and doesn't let me go.

The Encyclopedia

She pointed to where she used to live.
We were driving around. The guy driving,
I could see he wished I wasn't there.
She told me he was her cousin. Driving around
all day—we might have been in an American town.
To them, I was American anyway. She pointed
to where she used to live. With her two sisters
who were with us in the car, and their mother,
in a makeshift shelter at the foot
of a mountainous garbage dump. For an instant
it occurred me that the things they said—
about being sisters and cousins, about
this house of discarded tin and boards—
might be meant to fool me the same way
rolled-back eyes and feigned crippledness
were in the streets. Had they said it all before?

And she told me she loved me. And was due
to be married in three weeks. No matter
even if they had somehow been able to see
right into me, and knew I'd been brought up
along with my brothers by a single mother
on welfare, and had perfect memories
of living in squalid places, of begging for bottles
I would cash in for milk and bread, etc., etc.,
and of those parents in Nowhere, Suburbia
who would not let me in their yard to play
with their unremittingly average children;
no matter as young as I was, and as short
a time as I had known her, I felt love for her—
at the moment I was a light-skinned American
from a world of privilege and education,
and heading back to it, and it seemed
I might take her with me, just like that.

How had they gotten from a garbage dump
to a modest but comfortable apartment?
She told me how her father had died,
and now they received money. Her sad-eyed mother
asked me to come and sit at her kitchen table,
and watched me eat eggs, beans and coffee,
then motioned to her daughter to go with me
into their small living room. Such pure depth
of dignity in her mother, it hurt me. Without
thinking, I reached and took an old-looking
encyclopedia from a set in a bookcase. She told me
the books had been her father's. But perhaps
we should put it back—her mother might walk in.
Here, too, was a line I could not step across,
one that happened to honour love. She took the book
carefully and beautifully in her hands. I had
never seen anyone handle a book that way.

II

In the Same Blink of an Eye

Once, I was sitting alone. I had eaten dinner
and was leaning back having a coffee
before the start of my shift dishwashing,
gazing out across the cafeteria
at the people gliding out of the serving line.
I watched as a man paid the cashier
and took up his tray. He turned and faced me.
We stared at each other. And I realized
it was myself I was looking at. Not a ghost,
not a hallucination—simply myself.
And as soon as I had seen him, he vanished.
Once, I was sitting alone. Suddenly, I felt
I had been picking myself up, dropping
myself off, myself my own passenger
the whole day. I had decided to stop and eat.
I was on a whole avenue of restaurants.
Then, under the running blaze of signs,
there I was inside, standing looking out
at myself in my cab. And again, I was as soon gone.
Once, I was sitting alone. Once, I prayed:
If, uttering forth or at the point of dying,
I understand the way of things at last,
who or what will I be if I face something
that can do nothing but mirror back
whatever I have called myself? We go alone
to the alone; we do not know we go
as no one. We are broken from a no one
and remade over and over again
into a no one in the same blink of an eye.

Karaoke

A man is singing karaoke
in the Seabus terminal.
His voice is a ghost's
making a gape in the air
as it moves out
among the commuters
waiting for the next sailing
to take them home
across the deep waters
steely in the late fall light.
An odd voice, and artless,
but smooth, rich beneath
the hoarse, breaking surface
(the mouth it comes out of
palsied and awry, forming
all its words at an angle,
the face distorted, always
turned up off to the side),
it sings of love and love lost,
some sugary sad pop song,
yet really sings it.
One of his arms, wasted,
with a kind of flipper hand,
jerks across his chicken chest,
and every few bars
he snaps down and lays
his torso on his stick thighs,
still singing and smiling
while his head is hanging
at his wheelchair footrests.

He accepts a ten-dollar bill
from a woman, shifting
his mouth away from his mic
and talking, asking her
to take change from the case
lying open in front of him.
The song's tinny backbeat
and muzak melody continue on
without him, pouring out
of his portable P.A. system,
and out of the wheelchair
and the deformed body,
the ingenious half-machine
invention of himself.
Now I turn to him
as I put a pay phone down.
The Seabus is rumbling
into its berth to a buzzer sound,
and a couple of people
are throwing a last few coins
into the money case.
The sun rays in through glass
and makes the souls of everyone
in the terminal visible
for an instant, makes the souls
truly hear the wailing voice.
Listen to the reed, it cries,
and the pain in the tale it tells
of being cut from the reed bed—
how it sings of separation
from its home in any gathering.

The St. Alice

The Indian bar. One side for the Squamish,
one for the Whites. Lower Lonsdale locus
of an older North Van. Invisible now,
those soaked tables, the brass depths
of the draft, the brass- and stainless-steel-
bar-counter- and glass-washer-hued cold hearth
of unappeasable sadness. You sat down
as in a church in the comfort
of warily shared supreme discomfort.
Said the clipped, musical litany. Cabs flowed
to the curb to take people home
to the lower Lonsdale reserves, the Indian
and the White. The saloon doors
swinging open on the dark.
That moment of animal poise
in the shame of being there, human,
on display, the cells nailed to a cross. No one
looked at anyone else, yet each knew
where his or her self and every other was
to the exact subtlety
of antler-tips of spirit. Another beer,
two glasses, yes. Money left
on the table, but twenties not shown.
The washroom glare non-worldly
as of a forced interrogation room.
Last call, then off-sales for later.
The slender brown hand of a raven-haired one
is still reaching to her stinking dewy glass
as the server slaps a wet cloth across her table.
An old shipyard worker, his ruined hand
oddly delicate, and beautiful like her hand,
lets his fingers rest on his glass. All of a sudden,
Cezanne's apples are there, as if
about to slide off new surfaces.

Harbour Seals

They're driftwood or worn buoys—
now as they stand up out of the water
and stare towards the shore, they're living mineral,
like people with only rudimentary eyes.
And now I see one closer, see it dive,
and realize they're seals. Lifting slicked
black heads, disappearing back down—
they're seals. At this distance, soundless,
though at other times I've heard seals cry:
pure non-human cries that go
to the human bitter root. They're out
of some unknown watery testament
made of their cries, their wavering gentle
screams. Now I see a dozen of them
farther off, sunning themselves on a log boom—
solid blacknesses bathing lazily
in the long late rays. They roll,
all black torso like the mummified
Pharaohs, the immortals of the once-imagined
Egyptian ancestors of the familiar ones,
the Gypsies who flit past the edges of vision,
baptizing themselves in the dark nothing
along the savage margins. They roll over
into the water and are gone. Then bob up
new and black, being born again and again
into their blackness. Now I see that same one
swimming close, almost to the shore,
lifting liquid-like black and craning—it comes closer
as if I had whistled it up, asking for it,
and it had come, one of my lost ones,
my Gypsy dead. Seals all I can know now
of any of them. Seals that look out
in insouciant, terrible love—and can only
be other than seals because they're seals.

Sun Shower

Beyond the narrows and the bridge,
the sea is a lit-metal brilliance, the sky a desert-vault blue—

but here there is slender, slowly swaying rain
ushering light along the lanes of light's colours.

One sudden suspended raindrop,
a lens magnifying the air at all angles,

is the silent storyteller of this place—
where the sun lies out over the water

like a fisherman's tinted glass float, and the cast rays
net the world like an unknown, unknowable fish.

The Beauty of the Word

and my father's hand was trembling
with the beauty of the word
–Leonard Cohen, "Story of Isaac"

Rain and huge, wandering mist all morning,
and the mountain lost and closer than ever.

In the mist's lit drops, the primitive blade.

And the instant the knife
is raised above the son bound upon the wood
the son is saved—
and the rain stops and the sky opens.

The Abraham the rain makes,
the Isaac the rain takes by the hand,
the altar the rain builds—all disappear.

The trees look up, the always-bound trees,
the grass looks up, the always-bound grass,
the mountain sits solid, dark green and featureless.

And the sun, the sacrificial ram,
is caught by its horns in the silvery thicket
that the last of the mist makes.

And the air, its edges smoking and glittering,
the air that held an angel of burning metal,
the air is now an eye,
and the God who suddenly called out to the man
with the mouth of his own burnt offering,
the God hides now in the transparency of the eye,
in the beauty of the word, terrible and tender.

Lonsdale Quay

The little children come excited to the shore
where the unseen ocean ends, where the cloud-wet air
is flowing in and burning brighter and brighter.
Some run to a railing and throw popcorn
and beat arms like short chubby wings and scream
when the seagulls spirit the popcorn away.
Some stand rapt around a man doing a mime act,
trying to imitate his every expression.
Some dance the way toddlers dance, like little Chaplins
about to trip and fall, while a man plays a steel drum.

The mothers and fathers are here too, watching.
"Look!" one of them calls, pointing to freighters
being towed past each other across the inlet,
in the middle of long return journeys
between this place and Europe and Asia,
arriving and empty, or leaving and newly weighted
with cargoes of wheat and wood for building.
A child looks up for an instant, then turns again
to the quay-side where a row of tugboats
roped to a wharf bob in the water, close and huge,
and where, down below, seagulls touch on rocks.

"Don't throw them all," his father says to him
as the child ventures out into the dream of the air
with his package of crackers. But he throws them all
anyway, out and down, and immediately
attracts seagull upon seagull. Perhaps he will
remember something of this, in glimpses,
when he falls asleep in the night, as an old man
will revisit his earliest recollection, so far away
but all he has left in the great blank of his memory.
Perhaps he will fall down and down, an exquisite morsel
for the open mouths of dreams waiting to dream him.
The seagulls swoop down together, thrust out their wings,
all bright white, awkward-looking manoeuvring angels.
Perhaps the child has guided them here to the shore.
Now they fly up over the railing and wheel around him,
a haranguing flock after satiety and haven,
the air juggling sparklings around his head.

Heron

In the deep-cut, swerving ravine
the hour before dawn. Creek more spirit than water
pouring white down the bouldery creek path
at arm's length toward me and past.
                                    Out of the grey-dark,
suddenly a heron rises—a tent assembling itself
and, in a split-instant, collapsing
and assembling itself again in mid-air.
There it is, opening its seeming creek-spanning wings,
trailing its long thin legs, carrying its neck
in an S-shape, head held back: silent heron
flying away farther up the ravine.
                                    Is it the same heron
I watched once before—sensitive-still, slender,
blue-grey mystery alone in front of me in bright daylight—
until the houses, streets, cars and people
faded into the fringes of the light,
then reappeared along with this same creek
where it spills out of a pipe and flows for a block
through old backyards and into another pipe,
and I saw the still one gone? The entire creek unbroken
could be the heron's home, twisting
down from its mountain origins
of rain and melted snow to the inlet.

                    The heron
alights somewhere, disappears, and lifts again
as I come around a turn—and I see it again. And now
I see it at the shallow creek-edge, in an eddy
where the current swings out around a boulder and is lost—
all calm attention standing there, searching
through the creek waters' sunless rays.
                          It finds a fish—
the fish swims quick into the poised long bill.
The heron lifts, the dark tasting itself, the ravine
flying through the ravine—living sign,
secret heron of the beginning, morning bird.

In the Centre of the Day
for Jack and Florry

The first day of spring clarity of air—
it arrives as an invisible ocean
billowing through the sky, salt-scoured and clean
and brilliant-lit. In the centre of it,
at the far corner of the verandah,
the homemade rain-worn birdhouse on a pole
put up by the ship's carpenter-cum-dockmaster
who also built this other house
for himself, his wife, and future daughter
and son decades ago. Now the sparrows
have appeared suddenly like little prows
on the house they left last fall. There they are,
winging away and back, crazed- and tingling-
looking curvings of concentrated life,
inscrutable quickenings, crafts-creatures
of to-and-fro flight, and familiar
to the millimetre with every
nearby branch, fence edge, cable and wire,
and the birdhouse's doorways and perches.
Ever in motion, spurting out twitter,
they are almost impossibly happy,
they are at work bringing back the spring light,
as the man who put up their house for them
must have been in the days he brought his life
into port here in the house that still stands
March after shining new March. There they are,
the father on the alert, the mother
with the sparrow-light in the embryo
brightening within her. It is as it
has been in all the mothers before her
who returned to this same place. There they are,
in the centre of the day, scattering

their chirpings everywhere. There they are,
little keepers of the year's first season,
the bone-light beginning now in the egg
which they will build a nest for and keep safe
like a rare rhyme. The two of them bringing
the late March day into port, to the right
verandah and right birdhouse. There they are,
the little light-carpenters, dockmasters.

The Boulders

When the water barely flows
and the creek is quiet, it is a creek of boulders—

spherical, smooth, inscrutable,
unmoving yet seeming to move, vibrating, waving.

Now I know no sound ever dies—
no cries of the insane or tortured, no long outcries

of those lined up and made to watch
as others are lined up and shot to death,

no birth cries, no lovers' groans.
It is all recorded, stored in matter,

and nowhere more indissolubly than in strongholds of stone.
So many sounds, so many voices

await their release,
and the boulders imprison them

in multitudes of awful solidities without tongues,
in the conduits of ears stopped-up, heavenless.

Mountain Huckleberries

Pure red dot-spheres in delicate bushes—
I had forgotten they existed, and now, here in the forest
high above the city, I see they still thrive.

I might have awakened from a dream
in which I was a child, and almost everywhere I went
I collected handfuls of them, like the fruit of perfect blood-pricks,
loving the quick clean taste of the sour juice on my tongue—
and found the dream to be as true as anything.

And now it is as if they hold me out to me.
I will come back here, now that I know where they are,
with a container of some kind, and gather as many as I can.
I have heard there is a wine to be made from such berries.

The Gesture in the Creek

Sounds of birth spanks and shrieking
within the blank roar of the ravine. Now
where the current swerves and the down-rush
of whiteness flings to a level run and calm,
the creek is all makeshift swaddling-bands
from its beginning to its end.
                                    The gesture
is soft air—the clear sway-pouring
of the water, of the first matter, of the soul
that has just this instant been lulled
into the world and become water
yet still more soul than water.
                                    The reaching
of a bewildered unsullied one
held in the crook of the creek's torrent. Now
the tiny trembling star of this one's fingers
leads to a mother, a father, the way it will
to a friend, an enemy, a lover, a torturer.
                                    Ceaseless
new memory of touch. Gesture
out of instantaneous ravelling, unravelling—
transparency of a hand with the first touch in it
searching back to before touch,
wanting to place itself flowing in every palm.

Night Bus

A place to sleep, a depth-of-the-night
long ride from one country to another.
Milk run through desert stops,
finally nameless towns. The people
getting on, then off, in ones and twos,
moving up and down the aisle,
are an in-and-out breathing
becoming prayers I can't understand,
said softly somewhere inside me.
Unknown prayers, and people again,
ancient-looking, woe-papery faces.
They're illegals, temporary workers,
returning expatriates, visitors—
now setting out, now arriving
through small evanescent electric
glarings, trying to see; they put away
the things they carry, they settle in;
they gather up the things again,
and stand and learn to walk again;
I am nothing if not one of them.
They'll be elsewhere, they'll yearn
to be here—yearn unable to remember.
They'll weep, and close their eyes.
Now a stranger in the seat next to me
lets her sleeping head fall
against my shoulder. I don't nudge her
so she'll move away; she's the one
I've been looking for. Outside the bus,
there's the night's darkness; inside,
a darkness and the one who's more
than any starting place, any destination.

The House in the Rain

The house is on fire in the dark. The staircase, the door, the hall
are a fire echoing as with shouting and wailing.
The crossbeams and uprights, hidden decades
and visible now, breathe the violent air and smoke, and darken.
It is fire so thick, tree sap seems to be thickening in it,
the house the tree again from which it was cut—

the house in which I lie asleep listening to rain,
the solitary, old house that draws rain to itself
because it is solitary and old. I know the fire is real and is rain
because deep in my dream, for an instant, I am awake, and awake
because I have fallen that deep into a dream and hear the fire
while lying alone in a house so old and so alone.

I remember, when I was a child, I would imagine furnace fires
flaming up gently and invisibly from basements
to be piped into every household as warmth. Then one night, those fires
escaped and called me, and appeared to me, and were human and wild.
I crouched close to them, terrified to be flesh, desperate
to save the love shrieking in them, while I was made ash.

I must still go down the inside of my spine, following
the fire back beyond its origin to where I am altar and prayer;
there, a house is a way to listen to rain. And then,
if I awaken there, in a house, and within a dream of burning,
and stay awake, the tree of trees might break into leaf in me,
and the boughs lift me free to die. I will know how the light of day

is a dream from which no one can awaken
unless one builds one's life as out of the wood of that tree—
builds and builds it. No beauty but in expiring, simple things
alive in with what winds on and on through their dark centres
where they are ash, where they are exact openings
        of a rapture of brilliant air—
in the sound of inexplicable fire, of rain, and a house in the rain.

A Visit to the Dairy Queen

My grandmother takes my grandfather
by the hand, leading him into Dairy Queen—
though she's three-quarters blind,
she's the steadier on the feet of the two of them.
"Take my hand, oh Lord," my grandfather says,
"and lead me not into temptation. And help me
find out what the hell is going on."
Every week, he's more and more confused,
every week, he's less and less himself to us,
yet my grandfather's familiar sense of humour
still finds a way to stream out of him,
seemingly without his knowing it,
the way his urine now streams out of him
into the plastic bag strapped onto his leg.
"Would you like a coffee?" I ask him.
"No, I'll just have to go to the bathroom.
It's a bugger when you can't urinate."
"But you don't have to, you have a catheter,
you're hooked up to a urine bag."
"You mean it's automatic?"

He sways and falls back, we prop him up.
Trembling, bewildered, he's a visitor now
out in a strange ordinary suburban day.
Unable to hear very much, unable to remember
what decade it is, or where he is,
and between the anti-psychotic drugs he is given
and the who-knows-how-many strokes he has had,
unable to talk without slurring his words,
he's a comedian doing a drunk act.
Or he's an elderly clown, his running shoes
and jogging suit three sizes too big for him,
his socks constantly annoying him,
his crazy hair flying everywhere,

his nose bearing a large scab—
the result of his latest fall.

"What's your birthdate?" the nurse asks him.
"Bill."
"No, what's your birthdate?"
"Oh, March 18th, 1905."
"Your first name is William, right?"
"Right, William for short."
"How's the coffee, Bill?" the care aide asks him.
"They must be redoing the roof."
"How's the pizza, Bill?"
"Call the city, see if they need a manhole cover."
"How's the chili, Bill?"
"I didn't know there was a cow pasture around here."

"Would you like some ice cream?" I ask him now.
"Do they have ice cream here?
Oh yeah, this is the Dairy Queen. Okay."
He finishes the ice cream in a minute,
most of it running down the furrows in his chin
or splattering down his jogging suit,
and I clean him up, my grandmother,
serviettes in hand, trying to help,
dabbing away but missing the ice cream,
and I load the two of them back into the car.

Halfway between the Dairy Queen and Cedarview Lodge
my grandfather becomes agitated—
he wants to know where my grandmother is staying.
"At the suite where you used to live," I tell him.
"Where's that?" he asks. "What's the name
of the place we live at now?"
The questions go around and around,
the same two or three, repeated over and over
until, suddenly, he points ahead.
"Look!" he shouts.

We're passing a playing field by a school
where boys are beginning a soccer game.
"Remember?" my grandfather asks me now.
He's smiling at me, reminding me,
with impossible strength of gentleness and care,
of other days we have spent together,
and cheering me up, as he so often has,
making me forget now even about his own state,
the watery, childlike light in his eyes
perfect, still intact, still all blue sparkle,
keeping his pathways to me clear.

The Little Piece of Song

The Donegal girl from the visiting fair,
a little woman-child with a harelip,
is running through her repertoire
of the latest popular songs
for an audience of two or three
in an Aberystwyth launderette—
and flinging questions at me
in beautiful musical near-gibberish:

"And do you know Mariah Carey?
And do you know Whitney Houston?
And do you know Janet Jackson?
And do you know Bryan Adams?"

Her same-size-as-her mother arrives,
scanning the machines and faces
for possibility of launderette misadventure.
And her daughter reports to her:

"Farty p in datwun. Tirty p in datwun."

"All right," the mother says. "Go wait
outside the door and play your radio."

Not saying another word to me
now that her mother is present,
the little girl immediately dances away
with a quick endearing smirk
and a hilariously over-performed
coquettish turn of her head.

And suddenly she is out there,
facing the street, bobbing, tapping her feet.
With her transistor radio at her ear,
she is singing out the words
to a new tune she has just learned.

The little piece of song inside her,
and inside the radio,
knows all the songs ever sung.

The Prophetess

Again and again I made my way back
to stand there and watch her—
that glistening-faced fruit-seller woman
shouting out prices
in an outdoor market in north Dublin,
her lower lip swollen
to a naked pink baby
hanging from her chin.

Close-up, she gave off
radiant, unsettling energy,
wound up like a machine, not to be stopped,
staring out at some beyond.
She would throw the fruit
into brown bags and never break rhythm:

"Peaches 50p pound! Peaches 50p pound!"

Probably she was no more
and no less than a poor old Irish woman
grinding out a living,
and like practically everyone
in this lilting, shiny-eyed country,
sad but only half-mad.

Probably she went home
at night, as most did, to settle in unresistingly
with a TV set, a teapot, a cat.

Yet I also imagined her
to be one who had just missed true rapture—
one who had been struck once
as by invisible lightning,

and had opened her mouth
as a prophetess might
to reveal divine will, to utter frightened praise,
and been instantly disfigured.

The Green-Eyed Woman

Delicate in her tasselled
loose buckskin jacket,
she walks out of the bar
in the middle of a song,
past those whose stared-at
nakedness is a struggling lamp
and out into the street
and into a rain-music
that dies in the dark mirrors
of its pavement pools,
is reborn at her shoulder.

I go with her to a restaurant
where the light is the light
of a hospital at night,
light lost and waiting
to be taken back to a place
it knows it comes from
but does not remember.
I stare down into my soup
and see the colour of her eyes,
all my past and future
one in an emerald greenness.

I look up at her,
and she simply eats her soup,
silent, unaware of me,
or so it seems to me,
until something happens—
some subtle wild shift,
some perfect change somewhere
that is nowhere but here,
as in a rhythm-carried melody,
as in a never-heard rhyme
of feeling no one can keep—
and I am taken up in her
and back out into the street
now a many-coloured flower-world
in its pouring rain-light.

"I have to go now."
We are in the booth again,
and she looks at me a moment
and then slips away
out the restaurant door,
leaving the light still lost
and waiting, and me alone
with no knowledge of where
to take the light, or of where
she is out there in the dark.

Dream Catcher

Alone in my car, I had stopped
at a rainswept intersection
as if under tidal water.
The red-light glare blurring, coming
into focus, blurring again
to the windshield wipers' rhythm
opened a lost moment. I saw
a familiar passenger
sitting in the front seat again,
gazing ahead out the window,
smiling, very still, an old man
with hair flowing long and silver
and a child's eyes shining darkly
in the cave-dark of the taxi,
and saying, "You see here? Big sloughs
used to come in here where we are
right now. They would fill the creek mouth
then spread out, and be full of fish."

But I had let the nights on-end
driving interminable shifts
turn what I was into something
apart from me, so loneliness
and anger were radio hum
and engine drone, and cigarette
and grime and fuel and oil smells—
I barely even half-listened.
And when we pulled up at his house
and he asked, "Hey, come, take a look
at the new smokehouse I just built,"
all I did was answer him back
with the amount on the meter.
But he paid me, gave me a tip,
looked at me and smiled, and thanked me.

Now, suddenly, ten years later,
I was at the same set of lights,
feeling again how I wanted
to be swept up in cold waters
and endless travelling sea-salt
of purification beyond
memory, beyond everything.
That old man was likely years dead.
I knew now—I'd seen it written—
that those big sloughs had existed,
just as he had told me, where now
there was only built-up suburb,
and the creek I called McKay Creek
that ran beneath a busy drive
to reach the deep waiting inlet
had been referred to by others
with words that meant "saltwater creek."
I would have talked with the old man,
and listened to him, and told him
whatever I knew of this place,
if I had had another chance—
as I told things silently now
to the wind riffling through wild rain
around the car, the wind and rain
as close to a living body
as he possessed in the present.
If I felt I had changed in ways
that let me be more what I was,
it was because of him as much
as anyone. It was his eyes
on the spirit slough coming in,
the crystals fixed in his sight's net
and letting the good dreams go through
but holding onto the bad ones
until they dissolved and vanished.

Owl

Dawn a nullity at my side—
I find an owl lying face-up
on a cement walkway. Beautiful
small saw-whet owl, the round head
near flat on top, the thin white streaks
running up over the forehead,
the soft coat of rich brown and white
weaving delicate down the breast.
How is it that it is here? There are
songbirds that owls will come upon
almost soundlessly in the night—
if they find an owl where it roosts
in daylight, they will gather, mob,
and bring it down. But this dead one,
its wings folded in to its sides,
is flawless, no blemish on it—
not a wound or bruise. I take it
in my hands. Heart stopped, body still
slightly warm. Though no *too-too-too*'s,
strident yet tuneful, from the black
bill now. And still-staring eyes: eyes
brilliant, clear yellow, black-rimmed,
fixed in the sockets. How vivid
it must have stared through its nights. How
point-accurate it must have flown
through visions its eyes drew in for it
of undoings. And how astonished
and innocent-looking it is.

How idol-beautiful in the way
of some staring-eyed, storied one.
Woman flower-fine and faithless—
changed into an owl. Plot-emblem
of the invisible with its hold
on every turn of destiny—here
is its ruthless, uncanny energy
giving forth and at once arriving
at a face always the same
as this face. Implacable love
and betrayal and death looks out
in those eyes. In their encompassing,
wild centres the hour's light begins.

Your Keys

for my maternal grandfather

In the last year or two of your life,
you were always asking for your keys.
Every few minutes, it seemed: "Where are my keys?"
Bewildered-looking, and not remembering
you'd asked the same thing dozens of times that day,
frightened-looking, a child's desperation
shooting across your child's wide eyes.
"You don't need them," we'd tell you.
But we were wrong; you needed them all right.
You wanted your life back,
and were holding on with whatever delicate
and near-miraculous, harried energy you still had
to the days of house and apartment doors,
and imagining locking and unlocking
every minute left to you now
while you paced and circled in the always-unlocked
last room you'd live in, waiting to be taken out
for hallway walks or downstairs meals,
then impatient to come back again, and be there
alone with her again, just the two of you,
in the minutes you were still aware
you'd forget almost as soon as they passed.

And so when you were cremated, we had an old set
put in your coffin with you in your shirt pocket.
I remembered you years before—
before strokes and memory loss and dementia:
you and my grandmother
in the Sears cafeteria in the mall
having dishwater coffee and worse soup together.
She'd gone to get serviettes,
and you turned to me and said,
"You know, this is all I want. It's funny."
I thought not much about it then.
I was twenty, maybe. But now, fifteen years or so later,
I think that in your way you were handing me a key.
And now I wish you your ring of keys back in your hand
and all your memory safe, intact and shining,
and more—if there is anything more.

Psalm

That man with the biblical beard and long hair
whispering his sales-pitch asides—*Oh father, thou hast searched me out.*
That man passed out beside a dumpster—*thou knowest*
my down-sitting and mine up-rising; thou understandest my thoughts from afar.
That man fiddling with his rig in a park—*Whither shall I go then*
from thy spirit? If I climb up into heaven, thou art there: if I go down
to hell, thou art there also. Once, suddenly, while in a taxi,
I knew it was the actual you I saw at the curb—being helped
as you came out of a doorway. Was it the last time I saw you? What am I
of what I was when you had not yet become that man?
I remember I was eight and tingling with science and music;
I was the son of the prince; his eyes and God-dark beard
I wore like a family crest in my mind. And then I was seventeen,
knocking at your door and introducing myself: I was still
the son of the prince, and now with my own beard and long hair.
I eye you now from my fortieth year. You are there in my memory,
and in almost every man I see; even men younger than I
are somehow you—*Thou hast beset me behind and before, and laid thine*
       hand upon me.
My eyes go out from me. I hardly care whether they come back,
but they come back. And I have you there as in rifle sights.
I fire: you disappear, you reappear—*Thou art my path and about my bed,*
and art acquainted with all my ways. All I have ever said, and the only one
I have ever said anything to, is you—*For lo, there is not a word*
in my tongue, but thou knowest it altogether. All I have ever tried to do
is become a weapon beautiful enough to make an end of you,
of myself, and my name depart from me like an enemy—*Try me, O God,*
and seek the ground of my heart. All you are now is what I am of time.

IV

Nogales Prostitutes

All I could do while I stood there
dazed in the dim bare room
was wonder why the price of one
was five dollars more than the others.
The three sat down and faced me
in a line, nearly indistinguishable,
legs tucked in at their sides,
leaning on the heels of their hands.
All were both lolling and demure,
junior high school cheerleaders
on a gym floor of rough boards,
trying to look kittenish, cute—
but pockmarked, sick-looking,
counting out their smiles
and hiding in their pupils,
perfect glinting pictures
of a blackness that plunged me
into a strange sadness,
as if I had recognized
something I could not remember
but was desperate to return to.
I asked the man at his bar
with the rifle lying beside him
if he would sell me a bottle of brandy,
the amount of my offer higher
than the cost of the more expensive girl.
I had one drink, left the bottle,
and walked out into the afternoon,
the light glassy-red like a candy heart.
The rutted road now sifted me,
each particle of dirt a skull's eyehole,
the pure depth of a gaze
robbing me of any direction I knew.

My Hands

No one reads the back of the hand—
though the lines on the palm
might say something of the hand itself,
among the things it is said they say.
And the palm might be a living map,
but be read in numerous ways,
and tell a story more a question than a story.
Once, I went looking for my father,
and found him in his house on the water.
We talked, walked up onto a shore,
and got into his car and drove around.
"Same hands," he said, looking over
at my hands, then at his own.
Same small woman's hands, he didn't say.
His hands that struck and struck me
for nothing I had done when I was a child.
Mine that hit other children,
then men I would look for to hit.
And the hands simply hands—that wrinkle
and start to tremble with age, finally
stiffen and go motionless, that search
and find, and search again and find,
and end up empty. Except,
once, my father let his hand
reach over and rest on mine.
And he took my hand in his.
In the car, my father and I held hands,
he, thirty-four, and I, seventeen.

My hands now: forty-year-old hands,
older than I remember his hands.
The only hands I could have had—
the same as his. My knowing
what makes the two of us the same
aside from hands, my chance
to be different from him. Once, for a moment
my father and I held hands.
Our hands were the same hands—
hands that move through the world
and bring it together in its parts,
though they can know nothing,
as maps can never read themselves,
as metaphors can never follow
where they point to, as prophets
can never use the wisdom they have to tell.
Now, more and more, I hide my hands
from obvious sight. And long ago, I stopped
letting anyone read my palms.

The Shop

My eyes open on his effacing glare,
and on his father's shop, where he has worked
the eight years of my life in a job he hates,
where he leaves me as he goes away to draw.
And where I wander around alone hours
pocketing ball bearings, pieces of steel,
aluminum, whatever I can find
near now-still machinery. One night
it all escapes its drawer, flashes and spins
above me in an infinite system
of stars, and I wake and creep through a house
now the furnace of his anger.
                              Already
I am singing, singing out of a skull,
the eyeholes' pure unfathomable need
turned to burning blame, and I ask that the blame
free me forever from the kick and shove
of all imprisoned light, that the light pour
through me, and my father weep. Already
I am ushering him into the water
church and sanctuary lenses of my eyes
where he may gather up my hurt mother
and embrace her, and be embraced by her,
and the two become a changeless clear stream
glittering in the dark.

                    He traces a circle,
striding abstracted over and over
in precise fury around the front yard
while the morning gleams in the sham of grass,
and the new ghost I am searches through me.
The policemen on either side of me
observe him from the sidewalk. And it is
as if he has commanded them to stand there,
to act as his outward circumference.
And the part of me that can be nothing
but me is nowhere more than here. The flesh
is a molten dream, the breath a tool edge
turning the perfectly resisting light.

My Father's Shore

The tide flooding and flying heavily in—
all that has been, that is, and that will be.
And I have come here, I know, looking for my father.
And for an instant, I think I see him—
there where a wave is uprooting itself out of its own moonlit entrails,
like some poisoned animal, he is trying to rise.

But my father is not here. And if he were here,
neither of us would know how to welcome the other.

There is a sea, I know, suddenly alive at the tips
of delicately ringing grassblades of love,
opening into flower at the tips of branches, bequeathing itself to the sun—
but here there is only the sea lurching, and repeating its snarl and shriek.

The wind flings the grass down and yanks the gulls' cries.
The moon is a mirror in which nothing shows. The sea-foam flow
is a white death-giving blood. The glistening, massed, quick coils
of the wavecrests are the serpent hair surrounding Medusa's eyes,
which stare out of my father's face,
and wherever I look along the shore turns to stone.

Your Last Breaths

for my maternal grandmother

No more labour of breathing now—
the quick inlet tide stopped
that rushed glittering foam
up the sand at Ambleside
to anklet you as you ran
and played late in the summer light,
joy-loving child, surprise in her eyes.
No more, the crooning sound you made
like that of an infant or lover
as you communicated to us
with no strength left to speak
when we spoke softly at your ear
and you moved your head against ours,
all your awareness a caress.
Now the dying breath I take
knows itself as it is,
and continues your last breaths.
The sunlight on my face
which you will never again feel
because you have become sunlight,
the wind you will never again feel
because you have become wind,
the time you will no longer lament
running past you along the sand
though you still feel your heart
is a child's, a tone-pitch chime,
because you now sleep in time—
is the world your last breaths
make beautiful as they count breath.

The Man Who Was Never Cold

for my maternal grandfather

"Don't need a jacket," you'd say.
"No, don't need a hat. The rain feels nice."

And you'd stand there
on the frozen sidelines at my soccer games,
unfazed, smiling, soaked.

And at Ambleside Beach, loving a rare storm,
pointing to the brilliant whipped waves,
the wind bringing nearby tree branches down,
you were jacketless and hatless again.

But you were so afraid
of being out on the sea, of taking the ferry,
and terrified of heights,
terrified of being late for anything
(we'd be at the soccer field half an hour
before anyone else, and we'd sit in the car,
the park still deserted, the sun barely up).

So worry-wart-ish, so full of phobias,
yet you would stand and calmly thrill
to icy winter wind and rain.

Perhaps it was your once
famously wire-unruly red head of hair
(shades of it are in my beard)
that served you so well in wild weather
even when it had softened and turned sandy grey—
your hair had always been your hat,
your never-failing fire,
your orange flag in the sea wind.

Now, strangely to me, you shiver
at the slightest touch of the spring air.
I go, get your cigarette from the nurse,
and button up the cardigan you now wear
whenever you venture outside.
As long as I can I will keep you warm.

The Fall After You Died

for my maternal grandmother

Light brightening
the mist of low heavens,
the world's morning
arrives in the front yard.

Sudden brilliant
yellow gold above the house—
late fall maple leaves'
gold light smile.

When you lay just dead,
I was certain you pressed
your face up against
the inside of my face

like a child at a window,
looking into the room
at the one you had been.
And yet part of you

was already infinitely
far away, as if the one
that lay there had only barely
ever lain anywhere.

The mist will disappear
like all we pray will stay
yet be more real
than what we are.

But before the daylight
dries the trees again,
the sun trying to see itself
will look out of the leaves,

and the leaf-radiance
will be the last of what you were,
extinguishing itself
on its way elsewhere.

A Small Prayer

Two days and nights
after your heart attack,
you asked for a first meal,
a sip of raspberry Boost,
a mouthful of Cream of Wheat.
We propped you up,
held your head for you,
put a straw, then a teaspoon
to your elderly lips,
delicate and eager
as some tiny infant animal's.
You were so grateful,
and managed "Delicious"
and "Thank you," and lay back.
It was a last supper,
that first, last meal,
during which the betrayer, Time,
sat next to you.
You were already empty space
pouring into us
and starving us
who knew you would be gone
before morning,
nothing to remember you by
but our solitary selves.
Oh my holy one, my grandmother.
The hospital room
is a dark garden,
the avenues, winding streets
where Time skulks, damned.
The world you tasted
separates you from us.
Oh my raspberry and milk.
Oh my broken one.

Mouth of the Capilano River

They're out there somewhere: two among the many.
They'd sit here in their car, looking out at the river
and across at the mobile homes; they'd dreamed of retiring near the river.
Somehow one is my grandfather, wind and rain in his open heart.
Somehow one is my grandmother, standing on a stone,
watching the water plunge in circles, stretch over rocks,
frantic to reach the inlet—it plants its dainty feet
as if to stem the rushing, but the river casts its banks
and flaunts on. That soft bird cry is what she would hear within,
making her want to shout: *Stop, make of yourself a pool,*
a mirror for the girl in me.
                                        It's winter; the river's full and wild.
Yet the tide moves up the river, ocean and river water
passing through each other, mingling in the mouth. The gulls know
how the waters of this place can run two ways at once. They arrive here,
hundreds of them, just now, finding foothold along the flow
on a strip of rocks out in the middle of the river. They're messages
sent from spirit to matter and back to spirit again. They're standing
along an immense grey wing, the wing of the river—
living here with the gull-god, lost perfectly in gulls.

Circle of Leaves

On my knees in the cold grass, among the leaves—
the wind-brought-down, now raked-up treeful.
On my knees, reaching into leaves, the near-weightless
new earth of the leaves. I know I have run
from what I thought dragged me down, and regretted it,
and still, known none of it was love. And run
from what I thought a pretend higher world,
and trapped myself, lurched, and prayed for release,
and still, known it was not love. I am gathering
and gathering glowing fallen leaves. So many
fall out of my arms; I gather, and it is as if
the leaves flow away from me and back. I look up:
the tall, bare, black, cold-looking, rain-wet tree—
pure sign in the November sky, in the centre
of the empty purplish-grey space. Whatever
I have thought I had to do, I must do this:
I must gather the leaves, gather them up
here, in this place, and into a place, here,
where all the leaves that have ever fallen
from this tree somehow are. Here, where
I can never be anywhere if not lost
on the way between desire and death. And here
where I am gathered. On my knees, as I descend,

I am ascending, more and more leaves flowing
into my arms and away—influx and outflux
to and from the circumference of a circle—
and the tree above me, a Jacob's ladder,
up and down which go angels that are nothing
but green, rust-coloured, and green-again leaves,
innumerable leaf-presences. The tree haloed,
as if the light of an eye rayed from behind it—
eye in which the transiting leaves are the love
of the lower reaching up to the higher, the love
of the higher reaching down to the lower. Eye
almost recognizing each leaf, that light
shining from the leaves. And I gather up the leaves
and am gathered up in their circle.

Solstice Mist

More night on this night, more hours of darkness
than on any other of the year; the sun
more distant from us on its path than in
any recent year, and still: the full moon
fuller, more brilliant, coldly white. A mist
has been moving through here for days, arriving
and arriving as through a sieve. The rain
that might have fallen refining itself
for the mysterious work being done,
the darkness its own vigil in the depth
of the dead season—something so alive,
so delicately threading on and on
through the travelling vapour particles
and brightening as with impossible
gentleness, lit with what must be
originating in mist more than on
any other night. Some dream I had and as soon
forgot comes back to me now, inscrutable
as a pure beginning. Whatever made
darkness and light of itself says goodbye
to itself, arrives and arrives here lost;
wherever anyone is, mist touches them—
I see it as it searches for and finds someone
slumped on a sidewalk a few blocks away,
unable not to want to die, someone
lying in dirt starving somewhere, someone
checking profits in an office, someone
aiming a rifle at another, someone
admiring his own intelligence, someone
in a throng in an offshore boat, someone
serving drinks in his suburban house, someone
being beaten and stabbed repeatedly, someone
kissing and caressing another, someone

old, without anyone, taking her last breath—
wherever anyone is, whatever
made darkness and light of itself arrives
and arrives as in a silent, endless
procession making and remaking itself,
so many faces, all uncannily clear,
all unknown to me, while the brightening
moves with and through the mist. I think
of the one unknowable, unrememberable
dream waiting within every dream. The face
within all faces—the face that is mist
always forming into a face, the always
just-conceived child. Whatever I have felt,
it is kept in more faces than I can know.
However it is that the mist is here,
and wherever the mist is taking us.

Lanes

They are repaving our back lane, making a smooth track of blackness.
That gravel lane I ran in when I was a child,
where a thrown rock opened a hole in my forehead
through which I thought I could see into my brain—
it must be paved now, it must still be there, different but still there.
That downtown lane behind the old Carleton Hotel
where I was left on the ground by two policemen
who had taken turns shoving and punching me
after I'd exited the bar with a glass—it must still be there.
That cobbled lane in Limerick with Josephine Fitzgerald
whose arms I'd fallen into at "the dances"
and who had the most enormous breasts I had ever seen
("I keep them to myself," she said, and unhooked her bra,
greyish with wear but washed and clean).
That packed dirt lane in Magdalena, Sonora, where I turned
and was lost for a long moment in the sun, then faced
someone so beautiful she was God, and whether a child
or a very old woman or a young woman, I couldn't tell.
That silent whitewashed lane in a small Greek town
where, in a part of myself, I felt I knelt and wept
while the light caressed me with hands infinitely fine, not of this world.
That narrow lane in the medina in Tunis
where I heard the call to prayer and its echo in the hush
and smelled the urine and rotting meat
and floating cassia and sandalwood and myrrh.

That skid-road lane I stopped in front of—and entered
and gazed into at a father I had recognized
lying passed out beneath brilliant close clouds.
All those lanes still there—still half-hidden,
still connecting the same streets, one to another.
And whatever they have held, and for whomever, of all of it
in the end it is only the lanes that are still there, empty.
And I don't know if I have ever added up
to anything more than what I am that remembers a lane.
To remember is to see inside oneself for the length of a life
lanes that will have always become empty of anyone.
It is to be an empty lane seeing an empty lane,
an emptiness remembering an emptiness.

Acknowledgements

Some of the poems in this collection originally appeared in the following magazines:

Arc: "Night Bus" (Honourable Mention, 2002 Poem of the Year Contest)
The Canadian Forum: "Mountain Huckleberries"
Event: "The Prophetess"; "Brothers"; "In the Centre of the Day";
    "The Fall After You Died"; "The St. Alice"; "My Father's Shore"
The Fiddlehead: "Heron"
Grain: "Running"; "The Holy Rose"
Lit—The Little York Review: "Lonsdale Quay"
The Literary Review of Canada: "The Boulders"
The Malahat Review: "Nogales Prostitutes"; "The Shop"; "My Hands"
The New Quarterly: "In the Sonora Hills"; "Magdalena Dawn"
TickleAce: "The Little Piece of Song"

Some of the poems originally appeared in the following anthologies and chapbooks:

Vintage 97-98: "The Thermos"
Vintage 2000: "Karaoke"; "Your Keys"
The Edges of Time (Seraphim, 1999): "A Small Prayer"
Shore Lines (North Shore Writers' Association, 2000):
    "Mouth of the Capilano River"
Love in Four Positions (Leaf Press, 2003): "The Holy Rose"

"The Beauty of the Word" and "The Eyes of Travel" appeared in
The Accurate Earth, a limited edition chapbook (Reference West, 1997).

Thank you to Silas White for his superb editing of this book.

RUSSELL THORNTON was born in North Vancouver and has lived in Montreal, Wales and Greece. His poems have appeared in numerous Canadian literary magazines and anthologies and have won a number of awards, including first prize in the League of Canadian Poets National Contest in 2000. Thornton's other titles include *The Fifth Window* (Thistledown, 2000) and *A Tunisian Notebook* (Seraphim, 2002). Most recently, he conducted an interview with Patrick Lane in *Where the Words Come From: Canadian Poets in Conversation* (Nightwood, 2002). He currently lives in North Vancouver.